COACHING THE COUNTER

A Detailed Breakdown of How to Adapt Football's Most Explosive Concept to Your Scheme and Players

By

David Weitz

Copyright © 2019

INTRODUCTION

The Counter play is one of the most explosive plays in football. Made famous by the Redskins under Alex Gibbs, the Counter has started to make a recent comeback as teams move more towards gap schemes and start to use more misdirection in their attack. By successfully marrying gap scheme concepts and misdirection, the Counter play is a very difficult play to stop and can become a staple of your offense.

The heart of the Counter is that it is a Gap scheme. As a general rule, run blocking schemes fall into two main categories, Zone Schemes and Gap Schemes. In Zone scheme the blockers are going to be responsible for a Zone to their playside and work to gain leverage on their defenders to create running lanes for the ball carrier.

Gap Schemes operate on a different premise than Zone schemes by utilizing angles to give the linemen an advantage. The goal in any Gap scheme is to utilize down blocks to create a wall and then bring a lineman from the backside of the play to block any defender that is outside of the wall. In some Gap schemes, like Power and Counter, there will be a second blocker who comes inside of the pull and blocks the playside linebacker away from the wall. The runner needs to utilize their blocks by riding the wall through the box which should bring them to the Safety where they will need to make a play.

In the Counter Scheme we are looking to create some misdirection to help build our wall and then pull a Guard to be our kick block and an H Back to be our lead block. One of the best things about how we teach our blocking schemes is that there are specific roles within the blocking scheme. While these roles have default people that they are assigned to, they can easily be changed to provide a different look for the defense. We will get into this in more detail in the Variations chapter.

TABLE OF CONTENTS

LEGAL NOTES

OFFENSIVE LINE

The heart of any running play is the Offensive Line. The Counter relies on leverage and angles to help the Offensive Line in their matchups. Because of these angles and leverage advantages, many times a weaker offensive lineman can win a matchup against a stronger defender.

When we coach our Counter scheme we are focusing on a few key concepts with our Offensive Line. The first thing we start with is our base rules for our Gap Plays. From there we focus on the main objective of each unit of the line. We believe that when players know their goal they can then use all of the tools that we work on in Individual practice time to complete this goal.

Our goal is to always keep things simple. We want to be able to install our whole offense in four days. This principle of keeping things simple is taken to an extreme on the Offensive Line. Their assignments can become the most dynamic because of the stunts that take place at the snap of the ball. As a result they must have a complete understanding of their assignments so they can deal with any defensive look.

When we go through our install we always break our plays down as either Zone plays or Gap plays. The type of play will create the rules. One Zone plays we are responsible for out Playside Gap while on Gap plays we are responsible for our backside gap. Within both scheme the rules stays the same. You have the gap that you are responsible for, if there is no one in that gap you help to your buddy and climb to the next level.

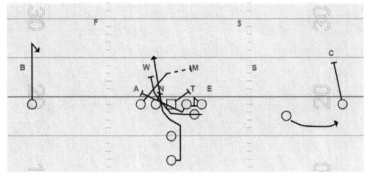

Counter from Trips Wing Formation

We then break our scheme into a couple of different parts. On the frontside of the play we are working to build a wall to seal off the defense on the backside of the play. On the backside the linemen have two possible jobs. The backside Guard is going to be pulling to kick the first defender on the line of scrimmage past the wall. The backside Tackle is going to be using a Crush Block technique to protect the backside and ensure that the ball carrier does not get chased down from behind. The final role is the H Back who will lead the ball carrier through the hole.

FRONTSIDE RULES

The Frontside of the Counter has one objective, build a wall. We are hammering this concept into our players. They all know that on any gap play they are building a wall in the A gap of the play and sealing off any defender on that side of the ball. This is done by following our gap rules and making sure we are protecting our backside gap.

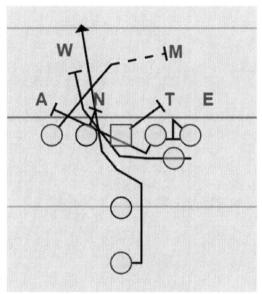

Traditional Counter Scheme

One of the premises we try to keep consistent is our rules. We always want our linemen to be responsible for a gap. This gives them a basis to start from and allows them to run the rest of the scheme. On our Gap plays the offensive line will be responsible for their inside gap. If there is a man in their gap they will block him, if not they will help their buddy while looking for any defender to show in their gap.

This means that our frontside defenders will have two possible blocks, a down block on a defender or a double team with their team mate. The footwork for a down block does not change regardless of if they are getting a double team. While they do need to be aware if they are getting a double team so they can adjust their weight distribution, we want to keep the footwork consistent. We tell our linemen to take their first step flat to guarantee that there is no penetration. The next step will come from their playside foot and bring them back to square so they can get movement on the defender.

Our linemen who have an open gap are the critical component of this scheme. While the down blocks are important, being able to add a second blocker to each defender lets us get the movement we need so that we can build our wall. The uncovered lineman is going to step directly at the inside hip of the defender he his helping his buddy with. He wants to use his punch (whatever tactic you may use) to lift the defender and get him out of his power position. By removing the defender from his power position the down blocker can now get the movement he needs because the defender is not in a powerful position.

The critical thing that the blocker who is helping his buddy must remember is that he is still responsible for his backside gap. This means that if any color happens to show in the gap he needs to come off the double team and wash the defender down. The majority of times this will be a linebacker blitzing the gap or a lineman stunting into the gap. Either way the defender is more focused on speed and isn't in a position of power so it makes for an easy down block.

The rules for the Playside Tackle can be a little different because he may have a clear shot to the BS LB. In the event that there is no one in his gap, and he isn't in a position to help his buddy, we tell our linemen to run their track. If the PST slowly runs his track he will be able to deal with any defender stunting over the top of the Guard's block. In addition, if the hip of the A gap defender gets on his track, he can hit the hip to help the Guard gain power on the defender.

The Center has a critical role on the Counter play. Because we are pulling the Backside Guard to the front the Center, by rule, is responsible all the way to the Tackle. The Tackle will help him by using a Crush Block, but this can be a difficult assignment. If there is a defender in the BS A Gap it's a pretty straightforward block where the Center will just use his down block steps to stop the penetration of the defender. Where things get interesting is when the defender is in the BS B Gap. In this situation there are two options, each with a strength and weakness.

The first option to deal with a BS B Gap defender is to have the Center work back to him. This is the base rule and what we start with. If the Tackle is able to get a good hit on the defender and the misdirection holds the End for a second this is the best option. The major strength of this pattern is that every gap is covered. If a linebacker stunts into the A Gap the Center will take him and the tackle will take the B Gap lineman. We will rely on the threat of the QB run and misdirection to get our running back to the wall.

While bringing the Center back and relying on a Crush block is a great way to base this situation, there are going to be times where there are some dominant 3 techniques. In these situations it's not realistic to ask a Tackle to slow them down with a Crush block and think that the Center is going to be able to get back to him. These are the cases where we will check into a cut call. This will be a call made by Center, although the Tackle can call for it if he sees that he is going to be getting immediate pressure through the C Gap. The downside of this scheme is that it leaves the BS A Gap open, which is where you will deal with a lot of blitzing pressure to stop this scheme.

Obviously neither of these techniques is perfect. Like anything there are going to be strengths and weaknesses in how you deal with any defensive front. The key is to give your players the tools on how to deal with them and teach them the strengths and weaknesses. By teaching them the strengths and weaknesses you allow them to operate on the field with the knowledge of how to see the issue and deal with it.

BACKSIDE GUARD

The Backside Guard has one of the most critical blocks on the Counter Play. He is going to be pulling and kicking out the first defender that shows on the Line of Scrimmage. It is critical that he takes a path that is downhill so he can ensure that he gets inside leverage on the defender that he is blocking.

We are big believers in teaching the holistic goals of the blocking assignment to our players. We believe this gives them a clear why behind what they are doing and helps them understand the goals of the techniques and the drills that we are using to develop those techniques. On the Counter play we tell the Backside Guard that he is responsible for ensuring the first defender on the Line of Scrimmage does not tackle the Running Back. He needs to do this by blocking the inside shoulder of this defender, but there will be times where the defender will wrong arm and get so tight to the LOS that the Guard ends up logging him (blocking his outside shoulder).

Everything that the Backside Guard does is based around the idea of blocking that first man on the LOS out. We want this player to be thinking inside shoulder, if the Guard is taking a good path for this block the only way the defender can get inside of him is to go so far inside that he gives himself up.

The path of the Guard is critical. He takes his initial step with his playside foot so that his toes are aimed at the down hand of the PS Tackle. The result of this step is that he is getting his hips pointed downhill right away. If his toes are pointing behind the linemen on his first step, he will create an open space to the inside and will not be able to get leverage.

As he comes down the line we want him to make contact on the defensive side of the Line of Scrimmage. This is a simple way for the Guard to ensure that his path is correct. The Guard is only responsible for blocking the inside shoulder of this defender, we tell him to run through the inside shoulder. If the defender goes around him to the outside, the Guard has done his job and the runner should be find to make it to the wall.

BACKSIDE TACKLE

The Backside Tackle has a critical role on any Gap scheme, but he should get some help from the backfield with the Counter scheme. By rule the Backside Tackle is responsible for any defender from him to the Center as well as any defender coming from the outside. This can obviously be overwhelming, so we try to keep things simple for him and tell him that he is responsible for the most dangerous threat coming from the B or C Gap. We use a Crush block to accomplish this, but it's important that he understands how he fits into the scheme because he will be asked to make a decision on who to block in a lot of circumstances.

We teach the BST that he is going to use a Crush Block and keep his eyes up to deal with the most dangerous threat coming from the Backside. The technique for the Crush block is to take two pound steps with his inside foot directly down the line of scrimmage towards the Center. If any defender tries to get through this gap he is going to collision them and slow them down. If he gets to his second step and does not see anything attacking the inside gap, he is going to hinge out and run out to any outside rush (normally the backside defensive end).

There are a couple of critical coaching points on the Crush Block that make it a successful technique. The first thing the Tackle needs to get his eyes on the BS LB and look at his demeanor. He is looking at the potential of him blitzing based on his alignment and body language. On the snap of the ball he will take his two pound steps and get his eyes on the linebacker right away while also feeling the angle of the BS C Gap player. His goal is to feel who posses the biggest threat to the Running Back getting to the hole. Ideally, the backfield action will cause the backside defenders to pause, but regardless the Tackle needs to identify and deal with whoever is the biggest danger to the play.

The second major coaching point of the Crush Block is that the Tackle must run out of his block. Once he takes his two steps in and pivots back out to the C Gap he can not stay in place. Instead he must move out into the defender.

By running out of the Crush Block he will accomplish two things. First, is it gets his movement and weight moving forward which will give him a chance to block any defender who he may be engaging. If the Tackle does not move forward all of his weight will be moving backwards and a defender only needs to drive into him to move him backwards and make a play on the runner.

The second thing running out does is increase the angle, and distance, that a defender will need to cover to get to the runner. If the Tackle does not run out of his Crush block a defender can run through his outside shoulder and make a play on the runner. When the Tackle runs out of his Crush block he will force that defender to go two or three yards upfield. These two yards are enough to get the runner to the Wall and ensure he doesn't get run down from the backside of the play.

H Back

The last part of the blocking scheme is the H Back. While we primarily use an H Back on this play, this block can come from a variety of different players that are coming from a variety of different positions. When you are able to teach this concept effectively your players will begin to see how they can really align in any position they want and still get their job done.

The H Back will be responsible for the lead block on the Counter scheme. This is the exact same block that the Guard does in the Power scheme. He needs to come tight to the wall and block the playside linebacker out. The goal of the scheme is to keep the linebacker outside so that the runner can ride the wall to the third level where he can make the Safety miss.

The first thing we teach our H Back is that he will need to take his time. He has to wait for the Guard to kick out the first man on the Line of Scrimmage so he needs to buy himself some time. We have our H Back take a jab step to the backside and pause for a count before going. In reality, they just take a quick jab step and then they go on their track, but we have had success telling them to pause for a second. This initial step is the exact same step that he will use for our Jet Sweep Series so it marries up well and causes a step of misdirection that allows our wall to form and stop the BS LB from getting to our runner.

Once the H Back has taken his jab step he is going to look to stay tight to the wall. We tell him to immediately find the wall and look to bend his path to stay tight on the wall. With that being said, if he gets any defenders coming through the A Gap he will block them to ensure that we get back to the Line of Scrimmage.

His path as he rounds the wall is to block the first threat inside out. We tell him to stay tight to the wall to keep his inside leverage to take the inside shoulder of the linebacker away. We have had a lot of success with this and I think it's because we are always talking with this blocker about leverage and keeping inside leverage on the defender. If he gets too wide on his path he gives up inside leverage and then he has to regain the leverage. When he makes contact with the defender he wants to drive him outside and stay on him to keep him out of the play.

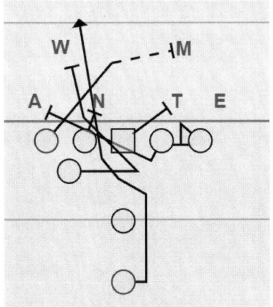

Counter with H On Same Side

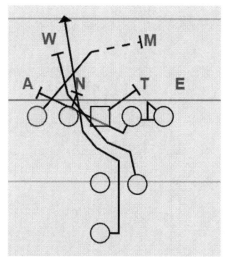
Counter with H in Backfield

The best thing about this scheme is that the H Back can come from anywhere. We have run it with the H Back in the backfield either lined up parallel with the Quarterback or directly behind the Quarterback in Pistol. We have even run this play with our H Back on the playside of the scheme, so instead of taking a jab step he actually comes to the backside until the Guard crosses his face, then plants and gets tight to the wall. This can really mess with the tendencies that defensive coaches develop for your team and can help protect not only this play, but your Power and Inside Zone schemes as well.

The most important thing when talking about the H Back is that he understands his role in the scheme. Once he understands his role he can start to see how he fits into the overall scheme and that it doesn't matter where he is aligned as long as he can do his job.

COUNTER GT

One of the plays that has been increasing in popularity is the Counter GT Scheme. The heart of this play is identical to the Counter scheme that we go through in this book. The only major difference between the two schemes is a simple responsibilities change.

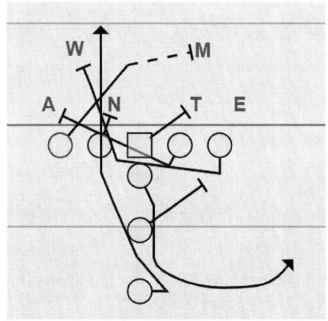

Counter GT From UC Pro

The Counter GT has a long history dating back to the days where Alex Gibbs was using it with his famously dominant offensive lines on the Redskins. In the traditional version of the play the backside Guard and Tackle will both be pulling to the frontside. Instead of having the H Back lead up on the PSLB the Tackle will now be taking over this responsibility. Because the Tackle is pulling he will not be able to execute his crush block to keep the backside of the line protected so in the traditional version of the play the Fullback will be replacing the Tackle to ensure the runner is able to make it to the wall.

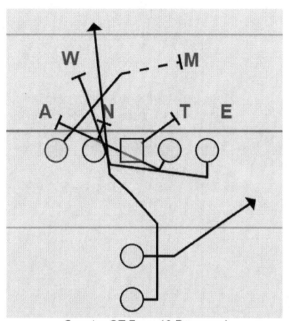

Counter GT From 10 Personnel

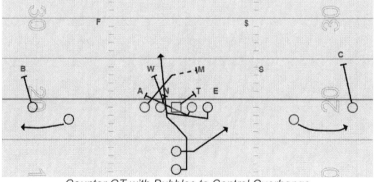

Counter GT with Bubbles to Control Overhangs

This scheme has been adapted to today's modern game by spreading the formations and moving the Quarterback from Under Center. We treat this play very similar to our Inside Zone scheme. This means that if the H is between the tackle he will be responsible for blocking the C Gap Player. If there is not an H Back in the formation the Quarterback will be responsible for reading this backside C Gap Player and ensuring that the defender can't make the tackle.

By removing the requirement of the H Back from the play, the offense is able to use the Counter scheme from a whole new set of formation. When this is combined with the threat of the Quarterback run and the misdirection that comes from the jet game, you are left with a play that is very difficult to defend and provides a great 10 personnel run scheme.

The Backfield

One of the best parts about our way of teaching our different blocking schemes is that the blocking scheme and the backfield action are almost completely separate. While there is obviously a hole that the ball carrier needs to run to, the rest of the parts the make up the play can be switched around to match what we are doing on the play.

The major elements we will focus on in this section are the Quarterback Mesh and the Running Backs path. These are the two elements that must be mastered regardless of the window dressing and different variations you may be using.

THE QUARTERBACK RUNNING BACK MESH

One of the most undercoached parts of any run play that is run from Shotgun is the Quarterback-Running Back Mesh. There are a variety of different ways that you can get to the mesh so we will talk about the mesh from three different situations. The first, and our primary way of running the Counter, is from the Pistol. The second is from the Shotgun with the Running Back in a sidecar position and coming across the face of the Quarterback. The last mesh we will look at is when the Quarterback is under center. If you are looking for more information about how to coach the Quarterback Mesh on all read plays I would encourage you to check out my book, Coaching the Quarterback Mesh.

From Pistol

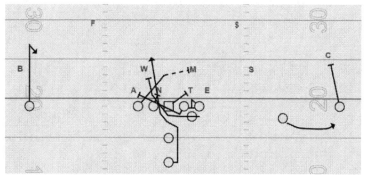

Counter from Pistol Backfield

We base our offense from the Pistol because we believe it makes the defense honor both C Gaps and helps to eliminate some of the games the defensive coordinators will play with the Quarterback reads. We really like this when we run Counter because it keeps the Running Back running downhill and makes it easy for him to stay tight to the wall. In addition it opens up the ability to read a second or third level defender (for more information about how to Install RPOs into your offense see my book Installing RPOs Into Any Offense) as well as the CGP on the backside of the play (this would be for Counter GT).

The Pistol variation of the play is designed to look identical to Power or Inside Zone. The Quarterback is going to open away from the play and get his hips perpendicular to the line of scrimmage while extending the ball backwards for the runner to run over.

The big coaching point with the Quarterback is that we want to always teach him to have his eyes up so that he can read a second or third level player. Even if you are not reading any players, you must hammer your Quarterback to keep his eyes up for a variety of reasons. First, if you ever want to make this a read play the Quarterbacks technique will remain the same. Second, by keeping his eyes up the Safeties and any backside Alley player will have to honor the possibility of him pulling the ball.

One of the biggest advantages of running Counter from the Pistol is that the path for the Running Back is so simple. He will come straight down hill through the mesh, once he has cleared the mesh he will plant with his backside foot and find the wall. He has to hug this wall tight and ride it to through the box. We have found that this is a great way to start teaching him the scheme because it almost forces him to take the ball tight to the wall and come straight downhill.

FROM SIDECAR

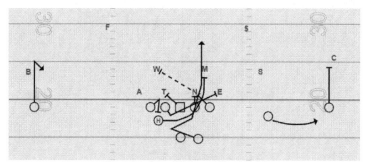

Counter from Sidecar Backfield

The Sidecar position is a great way to run the Counter scheme. While it does take a little more time to teach the Running Back, you gain a lot in terms of misdirection. This is especially useful if you run any outside runs like Outside Zone or Pin and Pull/Buck Sweep. One of the most important parts of running Counter from the sidecar is teaching the Running Back the correct steps. In addition he must be able to quickly accelerate and get his shoulders square to the line of scrimmage in the hole.

Again the Quarterback-Running Back mesh is a critical component for success in this play. A well run mesh will not only guarantee ball security, but it will also add to the misdirection and the ability to exploit defenders who are flying over to stop your outside runs. In this version of the Counter the Quarterback will be keeping his hips square to the line of scrimmage so when he gets the snap he needs to extend the ball to the playside.

The runner will be engaging in the mesh across the Quarterbacks face before planting and changing direction to get in the hole. One of the biggest coaching points here is if you are going to read any second or third level defenders. The danger is that the Quarterback will go to pull the ball late as the runner is changing directions causing the ball to pop up in the air. What we have found helps to eliminate this is to tell the Quarterback he has to make his decision early. If he decides that he is going to pull the ball he will take a hop step lateral with the Running Back to pull the ball. This creates a different feel for the Running Back so he knows that the ball is going to be pulled. This takes some time to master, so it's important to give your Quarterback and Running Back a lot of reps working on this scheme.

The runner takes a lot of teaching and he must understand not only his steps, but the purpose behind these steps and how they fit into the blocking scheme. We tell our runner that he will take three steps flat to the line of scrimmage. On his third step he needs to plant his foot, sink his hips and pivot back to the wall. He must accelerate off of this plant step towards the wall and get his hips downhill right away.

There are two major issues that our runners tend to have when they are running this play. First, they will not plant hard enough off of their third step. The average running backs will try to bend the corner instead of planting on their third step and making a direct path back to the wall. Because the Tackle is running a crush block, where he is going to be losing ground, there is a high chance that one of the backside players is going to be able to make the play as he bends the corner. In addition, if he does not make the cut sharp he will not be able to get his shoulders square to the hole and he will end up missing the hole.

The second major issue we run into is the runner missing the hole. A lot of times this happens because the runner does not understand the scheme and how all of the parts fit together. As a result he will overrun the kickout block and get tackled behind the line of scrimmage.

If the runner is going to be successful coming across the face of the Quarterback he must be able to quickly locate the wall and adjust his path to get on it. We train this in our running backs two different ways. First we make sure they see the play on film and how the hole will form. We can do this in a variety of ways and use any medium that works for our kids. Some things that have worked are to show it on video, run through the whole scheme without a runner at half speed so they can see the hole form, and even using poker chips or checkers to demonstrate the scheme for them. We are big believers that you have to reach the players where they are so we will use any teaching method that we believe will help them.

The other way we teach this is to force the runner to be under control and get on the correct path. We do this when we want to make sure the runner is going to keep the ball tight to the wall. We will find a wall or fence somewhere and set up the offensive line with everyone but the playside tackle. We will line it up so that the running back is right next to the wall and then run the play. This forces him to keep the ball tight to the wall formed by his blockers so that he doesn't run into the fence. We start by walking through the play and then slowly start building up the speed until he can run it full speed. The kids will look at you crazy the first time that you run it but it is a great way to get their footwork down so they are keeping it tight to the wall.

UNDER CENTER

There are times where you are going to need to get Under Center to run the ball at the defense. We are big believers in the Shotgun and what it allows the Quarterback to be able to see, but the reality of football is that there are always going to be times where it is more important to get the ball in the runners hands quickly and get the ball going downhill. In addition, we want to be able to run any of our schemes from any personnel and formation so we need to have a way to run it from under center as well.

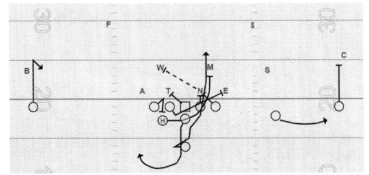

Counter from Under Center (Note-you could easily put H directly behind the Q in a traditional I formation)

From Under Center there are both strengths and weaknesses that you must compensate for. Different coaches run this scheme differently but we believe in handing the ball off to the runner on the playside of the scheme. While you do loose maybe a half second of misdirection, it is a much cleaner mesh and the misdirection and downhill nature that comes from running under center makes up for it.

The Quarterback has to work hard to ensure that he is selling a downhill run opposite of the way the Counter is called while still getting the ball to the runner with enough time that he can be an athlete and get going downhill. We teach our Quarterback to open opposite of the call and take a step with his backside foot at either 5 or 7 o'clock. This must be a big step so he can clear the line to give space to the pullers that will be coming under him. This deep step will also allow him to get the ball to the runner deep in the backfield. His next step is going to be directly back and allow him to start locating the runners pocket so that he can hand the ball off to him on the playside on the third step. He will finish the play by booting away with his hands on his backfield hip.

The Running Back is going to be in a position to take this ball coming downhill similar to the Pistol version of the play. This tends to let him stay a little tighter towards the wall and lets him come downhill with a full head of steam, which is what you normally need in a situation where you are going to go under center.

The Running Backs steps are simple and let him focus on getting the ball through the line of scrimmage with square shoulders. We teach the runner to take a step with his backside foot horizontal, opposite of the play call and pause. Once he plants off this step he is going to come tight to the Quarterback with square shoulders and find the wall. We tell him that the defense is probably going to bring another defender into the box because we are under center, so it is on him to run physical enough that we aren't worried about the extra defender.

VARIATIONS

There are a million different ways to run the Counter scheme. Utilizing both the traditional and the GT scheme the coordinator can create a variety of adjustments that serve to manipulate defenders and create a running lane for the ball carrier. The major theme of the play is that you want to find a way to get the linebackers to take a step towards the backside of the play. If you are able to get them to take a step towards the backside of the play, the wall has a much higher chance of getting up to the backside linebacker.

We split our variations into two different groups, the traditional scheme and the GT scheme. As a whole the traditional variations are going to rely on window dressing to get defenders to move more. The GT variations are going to based around the different ways to manipulate, control, and read the BS C Gap Player. As a result you will see a lot of carryover between the variations for the GT scheme and the variations that we discuss our Inside Zone and A Gap Power, which are both available in Kindle and Paperback versions through Amazon.

ROLES

One important thing that you need to understand before we get into all of the different variations of the Counter Scheme are the different roles that must be fulfilled. Every scheme has a different way to account for all of the players on defense. The majority of the time these are blockers who have specific roles as well as backs that are responsible for blocking or reading specific defenders. The counter scheme is no different, as a whole there are four different roles that can be changed based on the different variation that we are running.

The first, and most obvious role, is the role of the Counter runner. This is the runner that is going to be running the path that is designed to hit off of the wall. By default this will be the F, but you will see that at times we will also make this the Quarterback. This should be your best overall runner and a player that is capable of hugging the wall and getting you a consistent 5 yards.

The second role is the backside C Gap Player. This one becomes a little bit different because this role can vary based on the scheme. When we are running this as a traditional version of the Counter the Backside Tackle is the man who is responsible for the Backside C Gap and ensuring that the play doesn't get run down by any defender from the backside. When we run this play using the Counter GT scheme now the Quarterback will be reading this defender and holding him with the threat of an outside run. Other times in the Counter GT scheme we will use the H Back or a Tight End to block this defender. You will see various ways that we change the potential outside run threat to keep this defender away from the Counter Runner.

The next role is the role of the lead blocker who is going to stay tight to the wall and block the PS LB. By default this will be the H Back who is on the backside of the play. Obviously this is a role that we can change and we will use different players coming from different locations to provide different looks to the defense. In the Counter GT scheme the Tackle is now responsible for the lead block. If we want to run the traditional Counter scheme from a 10 personnel set we will utilize the running back as the lead blocker and the Quarterback will serve as the Counter Runner.

The last role is the man who is responsible for the BS LB. When we run this scheme we don't assign a man to the BS LB, but the players who form the wall know that when they get movement on their double team they need to be prepared to come off and deal with this linebacker scraping over the top. We have a couple of variations where we will actually read this linebacker. This allows the frontside double team to really focus on blocking their man and not have to worry about coming off to deal with a linebacker.

Traditional Variations

Q Counter

One of the easiest, and best ways to get in to the Counter scheme is by utilizing your RB to provide the misdirection and then have your QB be the Counter runner. While we run a majority of our 11 Personnel (1 RB, 1 TE) out of a Pistol look, we will motion the F up and have him come across the Quarterback's face. This is how we get to our outside runs like Buck Sweep and Outside Zone so it's a natural fit for our Counter scheme.

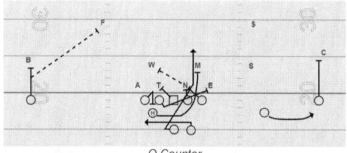

Q Counter

When we want to run the Counter scheme with our QB we will use this motion and ride hard across the Quarterback's face. This is really effective if you have been having any success with your outside runs. The Quarterback will take the ball all the way across his face before disconnecting and running the Counter Path. The key here is to get the QB to slow down and ride the fake. The longer the ball is in the pocket of the QB the more likely the LBs will be to play towards the fake and allow the wall to get vertical movement to create the seal. By getting a long ride on the Running Back the QB will also be putting himself in a better position to hug the wall and not over run the hole.

TOSS Q COUNTER

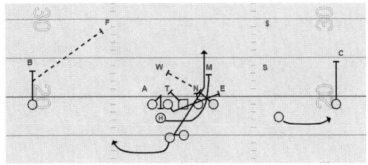

Toss Q Counter

A similar way to get into the same scheme is by using the Toss fake. Again this should match up with your run game, but if you do run the outside toss this counter can be an effective way to punish over pursuing linebackers.

One thing that we really like about the toss play is that it gets to the edge right away. As a result the defense is forced to react quickly to it. In this variation the QB will wind up, take a crow step and fake the toss before planting on his outside foot and running the Counter path. Again it's crucial to tell the QB to slow down. The longer he takes to get into the Counter path (within reason) the longer the wall has to form.

JET COUNTER

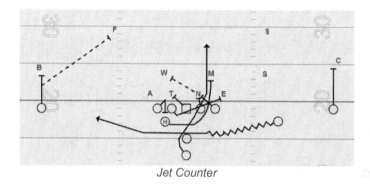

Jet Counter

We love Jet motion. There is nothing more terrifying for a defense than dealing with one of the offense's fastest players going full speed with the ball right on the snap. Because it's threatening the defense on the edge so quickly they are forced to make a quick response which leaves them open to a Counter.

When we run the Jet Counter we will tell our QB not to worry about putting the ball in the Jet man's pocket. While putting the ball in the pocket might be a little bit of a better fake, we have found this can lead to fumbles or the QB having problems and not being able to get to the mesh with the back. Instead we tell the QB to keep the ball tight to his stomach while keeping his shoulders square to the Jet man's path. We tell the Jet man to create a pocket and slightly turn his chest to face the QB. This adds an extra quarter of second where the defense is not able to see if he has the ball or not.

While these little parts are important, the major variable in determining the success of the play is the speed of the Jet man. We tell our Jet men that their motion is responsible for blocking a defender. If they go half speed they are going to miss their block and get the runner killed. We have had some great kids who understand this concept and do a great job of running hard on the fake.

JET Q COUNTER 11 PERSONNEL

This is very similar to the Jet Counter but if you are able to add your QB into the running game you add an extra blocker or misdirection. If you want to run this play from an 11 personnel set you can increase your Jet game by being able to send the back out to be a lead blocker for the jet runner while still presenting a threat to the backside with the QB Counter.

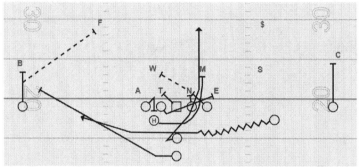

Jet Q Counter-notice how the role of F changes

When you are running the QB Counter off of the Jet there are a few subtle coaching points that can be the difference in a given play. The first is the Running Back's alignment. Because we base out of Pistol, we tend to struggle getting the F out as the lead back. We now tell him to take a half a step over to the side whenever there is Jet motion. This gives him the angle to make the play. In addition, some defenses will pick up on this and start to point it out. Because it is so subtle they normally don't notice that we do the exact same thing when we jet motion and run Power or Counter, the result is that they inevitably end up overplaying the Jet and leave the Counter open.

The other key coaching point is for the Quarterback on the Jet Sweep timing. We push the Quarterbacks to snap the

ball as late as possible for the Jet Sweep so that the ball
carrier is getting the ball and getting to the edge as quick
as possible. We want him to keep that same timing when
we run the Q Counter off of the Jet motion. He will want to
snap it early so he can get a better mesh with the Jetman
and you will have to break him of that habit. You want the
defense to have to react as quickly as possible so that they
can make a mistake.

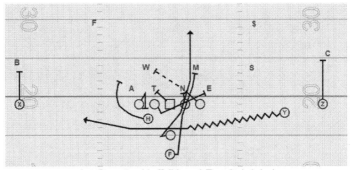

Jet Counter Huff (H and F switch jobs)

The other way to run Jet Q Counter out of the 11
Personnel is with a Huff tag. When we run the Huff tag the
H and the F are going to switch responsibilities. This will
mean that the H is going to arch around the edge and
make it look like he is going to be the lead blocker for the
Jet Sweep. Because the F has switched responsibilities
with the H he is now responsible for leading up on the PS
LB. The only real difference is that he will need to go on
the frontside of the play instead of the backside.

The Huff tag makes for a great change up when teams are
starting to key on the H Back. A lot of what we do is based
around the H Back and using him as a blocker at the Point
of Attack. As a result many defenses will be reading the H
Back to get an early read on what we are running. By

using the Huff tag the linebackers will be getting a false key. Whenever you are able to give the defense a false key it will slow them down and make them start to question their keys.

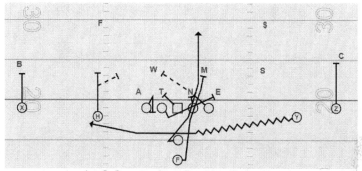

Jet Q Counter from Doubles Formation

One of the best parts of running the Jet Q Counter is that it can free you up to run the Counter scheme out of a 10 personnel set. When the misdirection comes from a receiver running Jet motion and you are able to run with the Quarterback, that frees up the F to be the lead blocker (just like on the Huff tag). This is a great way to punish a defense that tends to roll their Safeties with the Jet motion. Whether you are starting in a Trips or a Doubles formation, by running the Q Counter with the F leading you can help to protect your Jet Sweep play.

COUNTER HITCH

One thing that we love to do is read linebackers. We have found this makes for nice simple reads for the Quarterback and slows the linebackers down in the run game. We also like this because it tends to be an easy way to get the ball to some of our playmakers 5 yards down field and get them running against defensive backs. Many times if they are able to break one or two of these tackles they can set themselves up for a huge gain.

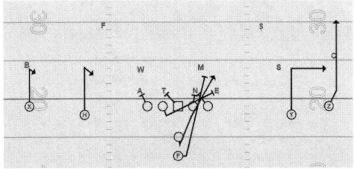

Counter Hitch Reading W

The best part about being able to run the Quarterback is that you are adding a blocker to the point of attack and should always win the numbers game. One of our favorite was to do this off our Counter scheme is by pushing our read to the second level. This gives us a chance to get the ball to one of our best runners while also keeping numbers light in the box.

In our Counter Hitch scheme we actually end up with an extra blocker in the box because we are reading one defender and using our Running Back as a blocker on the playside backer and our QB is reading the backside linebacker. As a result we will tell our playside double team that we really want to hammer that double team since there is no reason for them to come off until late into the play. This helps to create a nice clean surface for us to run to and gives us a potential for a huge play.

One key note for the line on this play is the Backside Tackle. He can no longer Crush block because the End could take a direct path to get to the Quarterback. Instead of Crushing we will tell him that he has that defender in man protection. This works within our scheme because we base out of half slide protection so this is nothing new for him.

SIFT

There are always going to be times in a game where you want to keep your Quarterback from running with the ball. There could be a variety of different things driving this decision. Sometimes it's because he isn't a very good runner, other times it's because he is a little banged up and doesn't need to risk a potential injury. In our mind, we always want to be able to read a player to give us a numbers advantage in the box. If we are in a situation where we want to be able to run the ball, but we don't want to run our Quarterback, we will run our Sift tag.

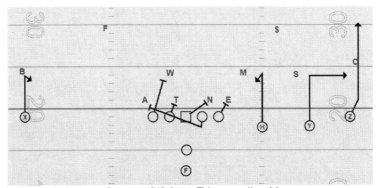

Counter Sift from Trips-reading M

We run our Sift variation from 10 personnel and really like it from Trips formations since it tends to take away the defense's ability to take the Mike and add him in late against the run game because the run is going away from the read. On the Sift tag the PST will now be responsible for blocking the PSLB and the QB will read the BSLB. This is a great variation to use against an odd front defense but must be run to an A gap player.

GT Variations

The best part about using the GT tag off of the Counter scheme is the ability to add window dressing to create misdirection and manipulate the read keys. While we normally run our Counter GT out of 10 personnel, there are a few ways that we can run it out of 11 personnel which allows us to add the H Back to the perimeter run game.

Bash

The Bash Tag is a tag that is becoming a staple in college and high school playbooks. One of the reasons it is so popular is that it makes for a very simple change or responsibilities that can stop the defense from dictating who will be running with the ball.

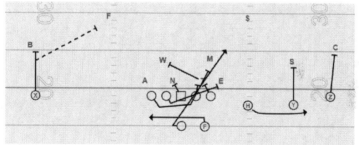

Counter GT Bash

When defensive coaches are preparing to go against an option team they will always have the conversation of who they want to force to carry the ball. A good defensive coach and team will dictate who will carry the ball by determining who the read player is, and then changing their responsibilities in the scheme. This can be frustrating as an offensive play caller because, when it is done effectively, the defense can stop your most explosive athlete from running with the ball.

The Bash tag is a great way to counter this technique. On the Bash tag all that is going to happen is the Running Back and the Quarterback are going to switch responsibilities. This means that now the Running Back will be running the outside running lane away from the counter blocking. Meanwhile the Quarterback will still be reading the backside C Gap Player. If that C Gap Player takes the Running Back, the Quarterback will pull the ball and run the Counter play with his blockers. This makes a great change up to slow down dominant and athletic defensive ends and outside linebackers.

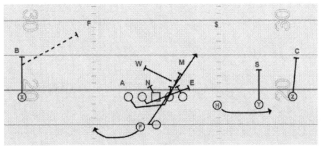

Counter GT Toss

Another way that teams have been using the same Bash principle but with a same side back is by using the Toss tag. In this tag (just like the traditional variation) the running back will arch wide while the QB uses his pitch motion to read the BS C Gap defender. Again if the CGP takes the running back by chasing the pitch motion, the Quarterback will plant on his backside foot and run the counter behind his blockers.

JET

It should be no surprise to you that we add the Jet Sweep motion in to the Counter GT scheme. One of the most effective ways to run the Counter GT scheme is by using the jet runner as the outside runner and having the Quarterback be the Counter runner. By using a receiver that is going in motion you free up the running back to become the lead blocker on the sweep. This can be especially dangerous if you are running it to the backside of Trips and the defense is slow to rotate their safeties over.

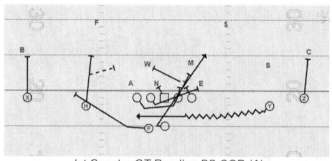

Jet Counter GT Reading BS CGP (A)

The mesh with the Quarterback becomes that most difficult part of this play. The Quarterback has to read the CGP with the receiver going across his face at full speed. There are two things that will make this play a little easier for the QB to read. First, the Quarterback needs to use the alignment of the CGP and the tendencies around him to get a general idea on what he is going to do. A lot of times you can tell from previous plays what the tendencies of the CGP are. The QB needs to use these clues to jump start his decision making for the mesh. The other thing that you will need to do is slow down the motion man. He needs to throttle himself down just a little as he passes the tackle. Once he feels the ball on his stomach (the start of the mesh) he can begin to accelerate and start to build up speed.

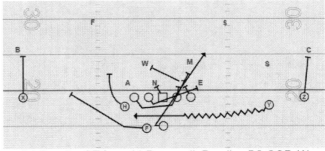

Jet Counter GT from 11 Personell, Reading BS CGP (A)

While we base this scheme out of 10 personnel, it becomes especially difficult to defend when you add an H Back and run it out of 11 personnel. Here the H Back will join in with the Running Back to become the lead blockers if the QB does hand the ball off to the jet sweep runner. Meanwhile you have the rest of the line blocking Counter GT in the opposite direction. This creates a massive split that makes reading the play very difficult for the linebackers and safeties.

COACHING THE QUARTERBACK MESH
A SAMPLE BONUS CHAPTER

The Mesh is the hardest skill in football to develop. It combines precise footwork with split second decision making. The pressure of making a correct decision in the mesh is a difficult position to put any Quarterback in which is why it is so crucial to develop a system for teaching and drilling the techniques necessary to make a correct read. Once this system has been developed it's important that it is repped on an everyday basis. The Quarterback must be able to react on instincts to make the instantaneous decisions that are required when reading the mesh.

In order to teach the Mesh successfully the Quarterback's role should be broken down into 4 stages: Pre-Snap, Pre-Mesh, Mid-Mesh and Post-Mesh. In any option play these stages must be completed in order to have a successful mesh. For offenses as different as Georgia Tech's Flexbone Ball Control Spread Option Attack to Oregon's Ultra High Tempo Air Raid Based Spread Option many of these mechanics remain the same for the Quarterback.

The Stages

Pre-Snap: Setting the Table

Pre-Mesh Position: Position and Preparation

Mid Mesh: Engage and Decide

Post Mesh: Disengage and Accelerate

Pitch/Pass: Feed the Speed

PRE-SNAP: SET THE TABLE

One of the most important parts of any read play is the Quarterbacks Pre-Snap progression and reads. The first thing the QB has to do before the ball is snapped is identify the Read Man. This will be the player he will read to determine if he is giving or keeping the ball. Obviously the player he will be reading can vary from play to play. The QB also needs to identify that player's assignment in the structure of the defense before the snap of the ball. Sometimes this can be very easy to tell, other times it can be difficult. One of the best ways to understand a defenders responsibility is to look at the players around him and remembering defenses must account for every gap on a run play.

While the QB is doing this it's important that he doesn't give hints to the defense on what the play the offense will be running. One way to prevent this is by having the QB go through the same process every time he comes to the line. This will make sure the defense can't ID which side the play is going to. Another way to make sure the QB doesn't tip his hand this is to not call a direction for the play but instead make it a check at the line. It can be stressful to give the quarterback the power to audible at the Line of Scrimmage. To combat this the QB must have a very clear set of rules to follow in order to make an audible. This, combined with confidence and trust, will allow him to make a choice and put the offense in the best play against that defensive front.

The footwork of how the QB arrives at the pre-mesh
position for a given option play can vary greatly from
play to play but each QB must get into a good Pre-
Mesh Position in order for the read to be successful.
The keys to a great Pre-Mesh Position are Ball
Position, Eyes on Target and Athletic Position.

First the ball must be stretched back so the running
back can run the ball through the mesh. (Note: There
are varying schools of thought here. I am a believer in
the ride method over the point method so I will just
talk to that.) This should happen while the QB is
getting his feet in their correct position. As the QB
reaches the mesh he should snap the ball back as far
as possible on a flat even plane. By stretching the ball
back as far as possible the QB gives himself a longer
time to make the read. The longer the QB has the ball
in the pocket the more time he has to make a choice.
Because the QB has until the ball reaches his front
hip to make a decision on the mesh he can only
lengthen the read by stretching the ball back. In
addition to this a long ride will make it harder for the
defense to see who has the ball.

The second major point of the Pre-Mesh Position is
that the eyes should be on the defender. We will get
to reading the defender in the next phase but the QB
must have his eyes on that defender immediately. We

tell the QB and RB that the RB is responsible for running over the ball since the QB is in charge of making the defender wrong. This means the QB no longer has to worry about putting the ball into the RB's stomach, instead the QB stretches it back and the RB is responsible for his pocket onto the ball.

The last major point in the Pre-Mesh Position is that the QB must stay in an athletic position. One tactic some teams will use to defend the option is to charge the mesh, others will send a "Blood Stunt" where two defenders blitz directly off the edge. The QB must be in an athletic position so that if he does get a mesh charge, blood stunt or any thing that makes him worry, he can disconnect and make a play.

Get the Full System Including Play Specific Footwork Diagrams Here!

COACHING THE INSIDE ZONE BONUS CHAPTER: THE OFFENSIVE LINE

Like any running play the Offensive Line is the heart of the Inside Zone. To successfully run the Inside Zone play consistently the Offensive Line must be able to get vertical movement on defenders. The goal of the line on the Inside Zone is to move the defensive linemen back 3 yards on any double team and 1 yard on a solo block. If they are successful the back should average over 5 yards a carry.

The rules for the Inside Zone are very simple and universal. Many running schemes have dramatically different assignments for the Center, Guards and Tackles. With the Inside Zone every position is going through the exact same thought process when they are determining who to block. This makes it easy to move linemen around and make sure that the 5 best linemen are playing on game day.

BLOCKING RULES

The blocking rules are all based on the playside gap. The base rule is that each lineman is responsible for their playside gap. When going through these rules it's important to remember that a blitzing linebacker should be treated like a lineman. If there is a player in their playside gap they are going to get vertical movement on the defender in their gap. If there is not a defender in the playside gap then the lineman will look to his backside gap. If there is a defender in the backside gap he will double this man up to the linebacker in his gap. If there is no one in his playside or backside gap he will ID the linebacker responsible for his playside gap and look for any potential threats to his playside Gap. On the snap he will step hard to his gap to deal with any stunting linemen. If no one comes he will climb to the Linebacker.

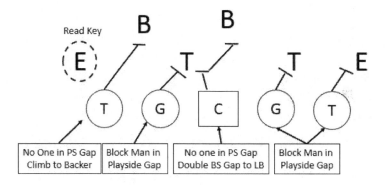

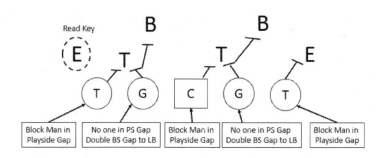

The only other possible scenario would be a defender lining up directly in front of him. If the defender is lined up directly on him he needs to step and assume the worst case scenario. In this case the worst case scenario would be the defensive lineman slanting to the lineman's gap. He needs to step with the assumption that the defender will slant to his playside gap, if he slants away then it is easy for him to adjust and get his eyes to the next threat.

SOLO

Blocking a defender in the playside gap is football's ultimate man on man battle. The lineman will take a 6 inch step with his playside foot directly at the defender. On his second step he should strike with his hands and look to cover up the defenders inside number. The traditional striking technique is to hit with thumbs up and wrists together on the defenders chest plate. Once contact has been made the lineman should run his feet and drive the defender backwards.

A new technique that some coaches are moving to is the double under technique. In this technique the linemen will strike the defender's chest with their wrists together facing the sky. The intention of this is to get the defender disjointed (hips forward). When a defender is disjointed (or standing) he loses all of his lower body strength and can easily be drive backwards. Some of the main coaches who are going to this technique are the legends Bob Willey and John Strollo.

*As a note-I will not be talking much about the specific line blocking techniques. I could not handle of the intricate parts and still cover the scheme aspect of the Inside Zone so I would encourage you to look at the COOL Clinic tapes.

Double Team

The primary goal of the double team is for the linemen to get vertical movement on the defender. The secondary objective is to block a second level player. An important rule to remember is that defensive linemen make tackles for loss, linebackers make tackles for a 2-3 yard gain and defensive backs make tackles for 6-7 yard gains. This means that if the offense can consistently block the linemen the offense can average at least 3 yards. If the offense averages 3 yards per run the defense is forced to commit players to stopping it.

In the instance that a lineman does not have a threat to his playside gap but does have a threat to his inside gap he will "help his buddy" and double team the backside threat to the next level. There are multiple techniques that are taught for this double team. The traditional technique is that the playside lineman will step with his inside foot and punch with the inside arm. Another school of thought is the under technique where (similar to the solo block) the linemen will uppercut through the chest of the defender while moving them back. The technique that probably has the most followers is the flipper technique. In this technique the playside lineman will step with his inside foot at the same time he delivers a blow with his outer forearm.

Regardless of the technique the objective remains largely the same. The goal is to stop penetration and raise the defender's upper body so his hips are disjointed. By stopping any penetration and disjointing the defenders hips the secondary blocker makes it easy for the primary blocker to overtake the block and continue to move the defender backwards.

One of the key things to stress to the linemen is to make sure they do not have a threat to their gap. In order to be prepared for any stunt to their gap they must keep their heads up and eyes on their gap. In the event that there is a threat to their gap they must snap off the double team to block the threat.

CLIMBING TO LINEBACKERS

If there is no player in their playside gap or backside gap the lineman will climb to the next level. Even though there is no one in their immediate gap they must again step to their gap assuming someone will stunt there. *By stepping assuming that there will be a player stunting to their gap they will be in a position to block the defender and will not be caught off guard.*

One of the tougher things to teach linemen is that when they step to their gap they do not need to be in a hurry. If they stay on their path the play will bring the second level defender to them.

If the linemen gets in a hurry there are a couple of negative scenarios that could play out. The first one would be that he overlooks a defender stunting into his gap. If the lineman is too focused on the second level defender and misses the stunter the play will more than likely end with a loss of yards.

Another possible scenario is that the lineman is too concerned about getting downhill and starts to raise his pad level. When he does this he gives the defender a chance to rip past him. Instead he needs to stay low in his duck walk position and trust that the defender will come to him. If the defender never comes and stays outside there is no way he will make the tackle. In this situation he has done his job and can continue to climb to the next possible defender

WALL BLOCK

One of the scenarios that linemen can face is when the defender is lined up outside of him and the play is going to be hitting inside. In this situation the lineman does not need a homerun block, instead he needs to make sure he makes good contact and keeps the defender to the outside. The Wall Block is the perfect tool for these situations. With a Wall Block the only goal is to keep the defender on the outside which will allow the ball carrier to run inside.

One of the most common scenarios for the Wall Block is for the playside tackle who is blocking a C gap defender. This defender is responsible for the outside gap so all the lineman needs to do is ensure that he stays outside and the ball carrier will run inside of him. The one thing that the lineman cannot allow to happen is a defender getting inside of his block. In these cases the lineman should start the play by taking a Wall Step. This is when the lineman quickly picks up and then puts down his inside foot in the same spot. By doing this he has maintained his inside leverage so he can stop any possible threat that may be coming inside. The key to this technique is that the lineman comes forward out of the Wall Step. Young linemen will take their Wall Step and sit and wait for the threat. This gives the defender the momentum and can lead to a bull rush that clogs the running lane.

CAN I ASK A FAVOR?

The big business coaching companies that charge $20 to $50 dollars for books use much of that money on advertising. Instead of overcharging coaches, we rely on word of mouth to help spread our message. By leaving a review, you would help spread the content and keep the price down for quality coaching content.

Please consider leaving a review.

If you would like more content and early access to upcoming books please visit our website at

CleanCoachingBlog.Wordpress.Com and join our email list here.

ABOUT THE AUTHOR

David Weitz is a football coach at Hamilton Southeastern High School in Indianapolis, IN. He has experience running multiple offenses and has been a part of two State Championship teams. He is active on Twitter as @DWeitz7 and always interested in talking football or answering any questions you might have.

OTHER BOOKS BY COACH WEITZ

Made in the USA
San Bernardino, CA
12 August 2019